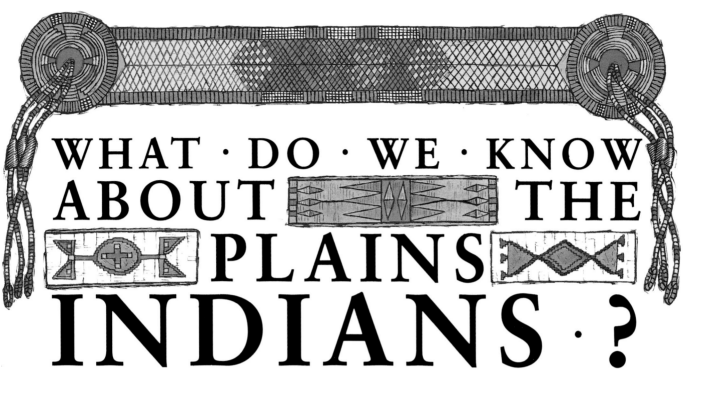

WHAT·DO·WE·KNOW ABOUT THE PLAINS INDIANS·?

DR COLIN TAYLOR

PETER BEDRICK BOOKS
NEW YORK

Published by
Peter Bedrick Books
2112 Broadway
New York, NY 10023

Published by agreement with Simon & Schuster Young Books,
Hemel Hempstead, England

Design: David West
　　　　　Children's Book Design

Illustrator: Ian Thompson

Commissioning editor: Debbie Fox

Copy editor: Jayne Booth

Photograph acknowledgements:
Front cover: Neg. #3264(2)5,
Courtesy Department of Library
Services, American Museum of Natural History,
American Museum of Natural History, plus Barbara
Feezor-Stewart, p23(r) (P. Hollembeak); Archives des Jésuites
St Jérôme, Quebec, Canada/Father Nicholas Point's Collection,
p41(t); The Trustees of The British Museum, p13, p15(tl), p20(b),
p22, p23(l), p24/25, p25, p27(t), p33(t); Buffalo Bill Historical
Center, Cody, WY, p18 (Painting: *The Storyteller* by Charles M.
Russell (1864–1926) gift of William E. Weiss), p30/31, p43(b); Bruce
Coleman, p12(l), p12(r), p41(b); Stuart Connor, p33(b); The Denver
Art Museum, p15(tr), p15(b), p26, p38/39; Deutsches
Ledermuseum/Schuhmuseum, Frankfurt, endpapers; Richard W.
Edwards Jr., p19 (Weyer International, Toledo, Ohio); Emilia Civici
Musei, Italy, p32; Barbara Feezor-Stewart, p42(l); Glenbow Archives,
Calgary, Canada, p8(r); Gloria Goggles, p12/13 (Fremont
Photography); Hastings Museum & Art Gallery, p39(b) (Peter J.
Greenhalf); Indian City, USA, p17(r); Joslyn Art Museum, Omaha,
Nebraska, USA, p24 (Painting: *Péhriska-Rúhpa* (*Two Ravens*), *Hidatsa
Man*, p27(b) (Painting: *Chan-Chä-Uiá-Teüin, Teton Sioux Woman*
(*Woman of the Crow*) and p30 (Painting: *Mató-Topé* (*Four Bears*),
Mandan Chief, by Karl Bodmer (1809–1893)), p36/37 (Painting:
Encampment on Green River by Alfred Jacob Miller (1810–1874));
Museum of the American Indian/Heye Foundation, p20(t); The
Museum of Fine Arts, Houston/The Hogg Brothers Collection, gift of
Miss Ima Hogg, p40 (Painting: *The Emigrants* c.1904 by Frederic
Remington (1861–1909); Pipestone National Monument, Minnesota,
p21(l) (Ephraim Taylor); Provincial Museum of Alberta,
Canada/Ethnology Collection, p28/29(t); Smithsonian Institution,
p8(b), p14; Staatliche Museen Preußischer Kulturbesitz/
Museeum Für Völkerkunde, Berlin, p16; Taylor Archive, p17(l),
p21(r), p28/29(b), p32/33, p34, p34/35, p36, p42(r), p43(t); Illustrations
reproduced in Catlin's *O-kee-pa*, published by Trübner & Co of
London, 1867, p28, p29; University of Nebraska Press, p31 from *A
Pictographic History of the Oglala Sioux* by Amos Bad Heart Bull;
Werner Forman Archive, p8(l), p38.

Typeset by: Goodfellow & Egan, Cambridge

Printed and bound: by Paramount Printing, Hong Kong

Library of Congress Cataloging-in-Publication Data

Taylor, Colin F.
　　What do we know about the Plains Indians? / Colin Taylor.
　　Includes index.
　　　ISBN 0-87226-368-1. -- ISBN 0-87226-261-8 (pbk)
　　　1. Indians of North America--Great Plains--Juvenile literature.
　　[1. Indians of North America--Great Plains.]　　I. Title
　　E78.G73T39　1993
　　978' .00497--dc20　　　　93-29066

· CONTENTS ·

WHO WERE THE PLAINS ·INDIANS?·

Indians were living on the Great Plains long before white people came to North America. The Indians' ancestors probably migrated from Asia about 20,000 years ago and settled all over America. The Plains Indian tribes spoke different languages and had different customs, but they all had a similar way of life which was well-suited to their environment. This book mainly looks at the Plains Indians at the height of their culture between 1820–1880.

GETTING AROUND

Plains Indians did not have carts with wheels to transport their goods. Instead they used the 'travois', made by tying two poles together at one end.
The goods were loaded on the back and it was pulled along by dogs. Later, travois were pulled by horses as shown in the picture here.

WHAT DID THEY LOOK LIKE?

INDIAN COUNTRY

The picture above shows part of the Great Plains. There are grasslands, valleys, hills, streams and very few trees. Summers are hot and the winters long and very cold. There were lots of wild animals on the Plains, many of which the Indians hunted for food and skins. The Indians had to adapt to their environment to get enough food and shelter to survive. And much of their culture, art and religion was shaped by their surroundings.

This Cheyenne warrior, Wolf Robe, was a typical Plains Indian man. He had a long nose, high cheekbones and strong teeth. Most Plains Indian men were slim and often over 5 feet 10 inches tall, and women were slightly shorter. They all had small hands and feet, bronzed skin and brown eyes. They wore their straight, black hair in braids. Plains Indian men had little facial or body hair – if they did, they would pluck it out.

INDIAN TERRITORIES

Look at the map on the right to see where different tribes lived. There were about twenty Plains tribes made up of 4,000–15,000 people. The total population in about 1800 was 120,000. Some Plains Indian tribes were semi-settled, living in villages along rivers like the Missouri. Other tribes were nomadic. They roamed across the Plains, living in tepees and following the huge herds of buffalo which they hunted. By 1650, some southern Plains tribes had acquired horses from Spanish settlers which made travel easier and quicker.

THE GREAT PLAINS

As the map below shows, the Great Plains are found in the heartland of North America. The Plains cover approximately 780,000 square miles with the Saskatchewan River to the north, the Rio Grande to the south, the Mississippi River to the east and the Rocky Mountains to the west.

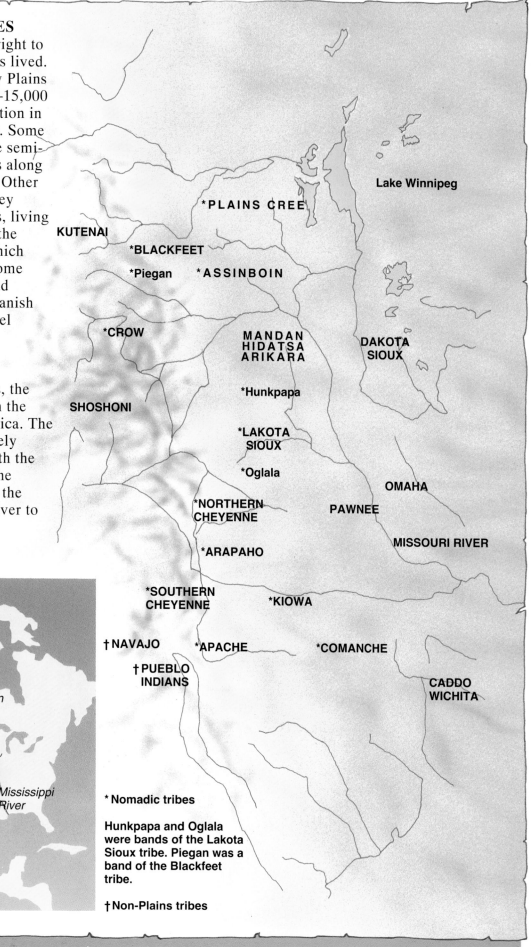

Lake Winnipeg

*PLAINS CREE

KUTENAI

*BLACKFEET

*Piegan   *ASSINBOIN

*CROW

MANDAN
HIDATSA
ARIKARA

DAKOTA
SIOUX

*Hunkpapa

SHOSHONI

*LAKOTA
SIOUX

*Oglala

OMAHA

*NORTHERN
CHEYENNE

PAWNEE

*ARAPAHO

MISSOURI RIVER

*SOUTHERN
CHEYENNE   *KIOWA

†NAVAJO   *APACHE   *COMANCHE

†PUEBLO
INDIANS

CADDO
WICHITA

*Nomadic tribes

Hunkpapa and Oglala were bands of the Lakota Sioux tribe. Piegan was a band of the Blackfeet tribe.

†Non-Plains tribes

Saskatchewan River

Great Plains

Rocky Mountains

Mississippi River

Rio Grande

9

TIMELINE

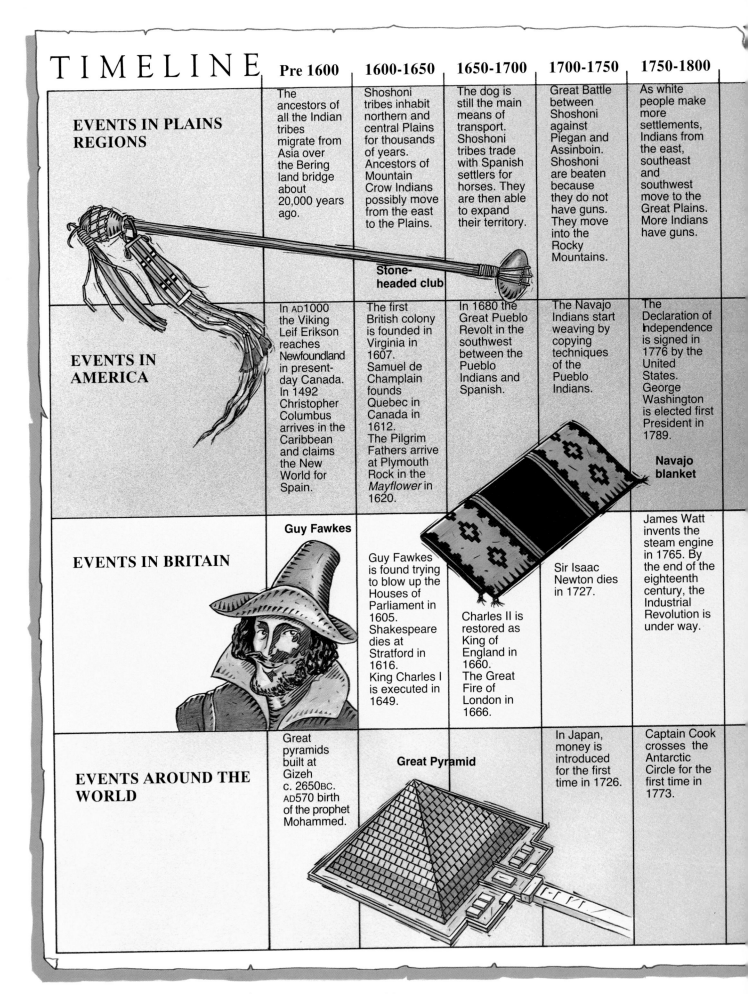

	Pre 1600	1600-1650	1650-1700	1700-1750	1750-1800
EVENTS IN PLAINS REGIONS	The ancestors of all the Indian tribes migrate from Asia over the Bering land bridge about 20,000 years ago.	Shoshoni tribes inhabit northern and central Plains for thousands of years. Ancestors of Mountain Crow Indians possibly move from the east to the Plains.	The dog is still the main means of transport. Shoshoni tribes trade with Spanish settlers for horses. They are then able to expand their territory.	Great Battle between Shoshoni against Piegan and Assinboin. Shoshoni are beaten because they do not have guns. They move into the Rocky Mountains.	As white people make more settlements, Indians from the east, southeast and southwest move to the Great Plains. More Indians have guns.
EVENTS IN AMERICA	In AD1000 the Viking Leif Erikson reaches Newfoundland in present-day Canada. In 1492 Christopher Columbus arrives in the Caribbean and claims the New World for Spain.	The first British colony is founded in Virginia in 1607. Samuel de Champlain founds Quebec in Canada in 1612. The Pilgrim Fathers arrive at Plymouth Rock in the *Mayflower* in 1620.	In 1680 the Great Pueblo Revolt in the southwest between the Pueblo Indians and Spanish.	The Navajo Indians start weaving by copying techniques of the Pueblo Indians.	The Declaration of Independence is signed in 1776 by the United States. George Washington is elected first President in 1789.
EVENTS IN BRITAIN		Guy Fawkes is found trying to blow up the Houses of Parliament in 1605. Shakespeare dies at Stratford in 1616. King Charles I is executed in 1649.	Charles II is restored as King of England in 1660. The Great Fire of London in 1666.	Sir Isaac Newton dies in 1727.	James Watt invents the steam engine in 1765. By the end of the eighteenth century, the Industrial Revolution is under way.
EVENTS AROUND THE WORLD	Great pyramids built at Gizeh c. 2650BC. AD570 birth of the prophet Mohammed.			In Japan, money is introduced for the first time in 1726.	Captain Cook crosses the Antarctic Circle for the first time in 1773.

Stone-headed club

Navajo blanket

Guy Fawkes

Great Pyramid

1800-1850	1850-1900	1900-1950	1950-1990	1990s
The major period of the Plains Indians' way of life. The nomadic tribes depend on horses and the buffalo. White explorers and artists begin to visit the Indians.	White settlers move across the Plains and some fight with tribes. Cheyenne and Sioux win Battle of Little Big Horn in 1876.	Plains Indians are forced to live on reservations. Buffalo are all but exterminated by hide hunters and the Indians' way of life is destroyed.	Oil, coal and gas found on Indian reservations make them more independent. Indian tribes begin to assert themselves and their way of life.	Many Indians are now well educated and go to university. They assert their rights and revive old traditions.
James Fenimore Cooper's novel *The Last of the Mohicans* is published in 1823. Canada is granted self-government in 1841.	1852 Harriet Beecher Stowe's novel *Uncle Tom's Cabin* shows cruelty of slavery. Henry Longfellow's poem *Hiawatha* is published in 1855. 1861-1865 American Civil War.	The Panama Canal linking the Atlantic and Pacific Oceans is built 1904-1914. The Wall Street Crash of 1929 starts the Great Depression of the 1930s.	President John F. Kennedy is assassinated in 1963. Neil Armstrong becomes the first man to walk on the moon in 1969. President Richard Nixon resigns over the Watergate scandal in 1974.	Bill Clinton becomes President in 1993.
Battle of Waterloo in 1815 marks the final defeat of Napoleon I. Queen Victoria comes to the British throne in 1837.	Outbreak of the Crimean War is followed by the disastrous Charge of the Light Brigade in 1854.	First World War breaks out in Europe in 1914. Logie Baird displays color television in 1929.	Festival of Britain is opened by King George VI in 1951. The Beatles have their first hit *Love Me Do* in 1962.	The Conservative Party in the United Kingdom win their fourth election in 1992.
Charles Darwin studies wildlife on the Galapagos Islands in 1835. His work leads him to publish *The Origin of Species* in 1859.	Over 55 million people leave Europe to settle in America in the second half of the nineteenth century.	Global war, which starts in Europe in 1939, is ended when the first atomic bombs are dropped on Hiroshima and Nagasaki in Japan in August 1945.	In 1952, a fish called a coelacanth is caught near Madagascar. It was thought to have been extinct for 50 million years.	Civil War rages in Yugoslavia.

Pipe tomahawk

Atomic bomb

Most of the Plains Indians tribes described in this book came from northern and eastern America and settled on the Great Plains from about 1730. They spoke about six different languages – Algonquian, Athabaskan, Caddoan, Iowan, Siouan and Uto-Aztecan – with several different dialects too. Although each tribe had its own customs and traditions, they all shared a similar way of life. The lifestyle of the Plains Indians changed dramatically from 1740 as their contact with white people increased.

Some people call Plains Indians 'Native Americans', but they prefer to be known by the name of their tribe. For example, there are many Sioux tribes. The western Sioux call themselves Lakota and the eastern, Dakota. Within the tribes are smaller bands or groups.

HORSES

Horses were taken to North America by the Spaniards in 1541. They traded them to the Comanche who then traded them to other tribes living on the Great Plains. The Lakota Indians called horses *Shonka Wakan* which means 'medicine dog'.

·WHAT· ·FOOD· DID THEY ·EAT?·

Indian tribes had to hunt, collect or grow all their food. They also had to develop ways to preserve and store meat and vegetables for the winter when food was scarce. Some tribes, like the Mandan and Hidatsa, farmed various crops such as maize, beans and pumpkins. But nomadic tribes like the Cheyenne or Comanche mainly hunted wild animals and collected wild fruits and vegetables. The prairie turnip was a very important wild vegetable. It was dug up using a special stick, then it could be dried and saved for the winter. Food was often traded between tribes.

DIFFERENT FOODS

This large picture shows many kinds of Indian foods prepared by Gloria Goggles of the Arapaho tribe in Wyoming. You can see the prairie turnips, dried and tied in strings. These will keep for several years as long as they do not get damp. There are ears of maize and bowls of dried and fresh plums too. Some of the meat has been dried, and some has been mixed with herbs and stuffed to make a kind of sausage.

BUFFALO

The Plains Indians depended on the buffalo, which are the largest mammals in North America. They are about 6½ feet tall and weigh up to 2,200 pounds. Before the Indians had horses, they captured buffalo in V-shaped pens or drove them over cliffs to kill them. The Indians also hunted prong-horned antelopes in a similar way.

Prong-horned antelope

PLAINS PLANTS AND ANIMALS

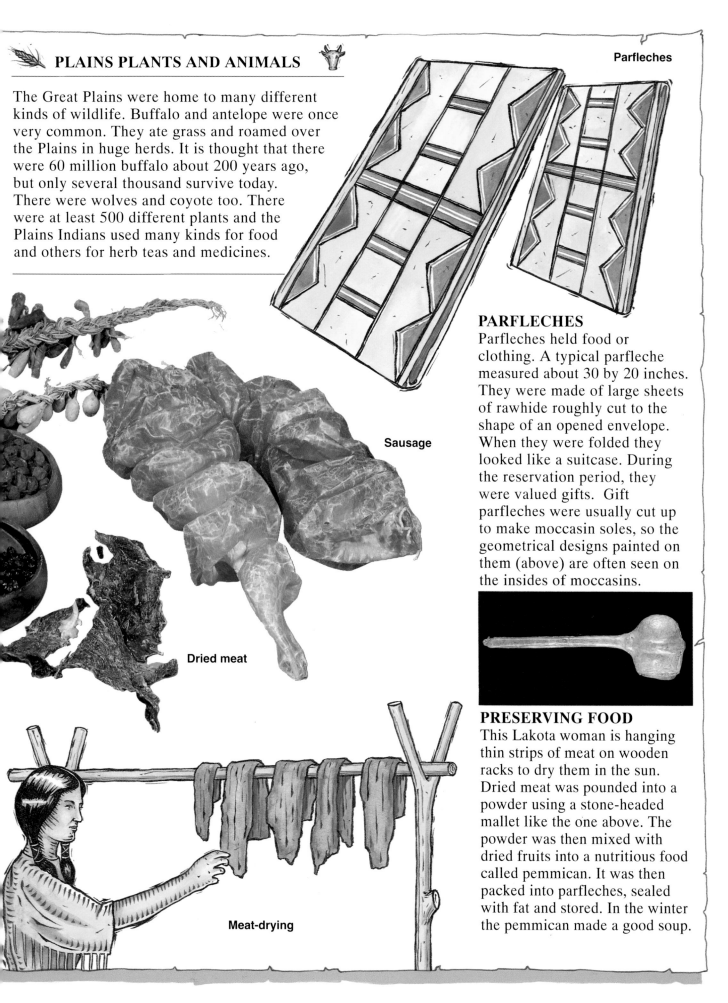

The Great Plains were home to many different kinds of wildlife. Buffalo and antelope were once very common. They ate grass and roamed over the Plains in huge herds. It is thought that there were 60 million buffalo about 200 years ago, but only several thousand survive today. There were wolves and coyote too. There were at least 500 different plants and the Plains Indians used many kinds for food and others for herb teas and medicines.

Parfleches

Sausage

Dried meat

Meat-drying

PARFLECHES
Parfleches held food or clothing. A typical parfleche measured about 30 by 20 inches. They were made of large sheets of rawhide roughly cut to the shape of an opened envelope. When they were folded they looked like a suitcase. During the reservation period, they were valued gifts. Gift parfleches were usually cut up to make moccasin soles, so the geometrical designs painted on them (above) are often seen on the insides of moccasins.

PRESERVING FOOD
This Lakota woman is hanging thin strips of meat on wooden racks to dry them in the sun. Dried meat was pounded into a powder using a stone-headed mallet like the one above. The powder was then mixed with dried fruits into a nutritious food called pemmican. It was then packed into parfleches, sealed with fat and stored. In the winter the pemmican made a good soup.

· W H A T · · W A S · FAMILY LIFE · L I K E ? ·

The family was a very important part of the Plains Indians' way of life. A young man had to prove he could provide food and transport for his family by going on several hunts and raiding his tribe's enemy for horses. Only then could he think about marrying. An Indian man could have as many wives as he wished, but many only had one. A few men had more than three wives who were often sisters because they felt sisters would not squabble. Having children was very important to the Plains Indians. Mothers were always with their babies, but other family members also helped to care for the children, especially grandmothers.

FATHERS AND FAMILIES

In the semi-settled tribes like the Omaha, men often looked after their children. Fathers and grandfathers played with or soothed unhappy children. In this photograph, taken around 1890, a Cheyenne father and his sons pose in their traditional clothes made by their mother or grandmother. The older boy looks rather startled by the flash.

 GUARDIAN SPIRITS

At the age of fourteen, a Plains Indian boy would leave his camp alone to look for his guardian spirit to protect and help him through his life. He stayed alone for four days and nights on a high hill, praying and waiting for the spirit to come to him. Some boys had dreams where they saw animal spirits, such as buffalo, bears, wolves and eagles, who would pass on their strengths and skills. Often the visions were confusing and one of the tribe's holy men would have to interpret them. Boys often wore an amulet to represent their guardian spirit.

A PLAINS INDIAN CRADLE

When a new baby was born, the grandparents usually made a cradle. Cradles like this one were made with two wooden boards about 4 feet long. Rawhide was used to join the boards together, then a soft animal skin bag was stretched over the top. The baby could then be carried safely and comfortably on horseback. The bag's beautiful decorations often were not completed until the baby was born so that family designs could be added to show if the baby was a boy or a girl.

BALL GAMES

Boys often played a game called shinny that later became ice hockey. They used a long curved wooden stick to knock a ball over a goal line. The ball was originally made of baked clay covered with buckskin. The ball shown above has been completely covered with beautiful beadwork. The boys developed fitness, speed and skill playing shinny, which would be useful when they grew up to be hunters. This popular game was played by Indians all over America.

DOLLS

The dolls on the left were made in about 1880 for a Lakota girl. Dolls were normally made of soft buckskin. Their faces were painted or sewn in beadwork and their hair came from a lock of a relative's hair. Dolls were dressed in the typical clothes of the tribe like the woman's beaded dress or the man's shirt.

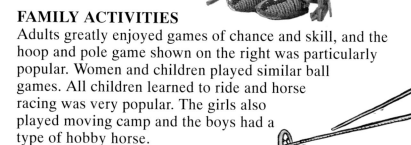

Hoop and pole game

FAMILY ACTIVITIES

Adults greatly enjoyed games of chance and skill, and the hoop and pole game shown on the right was particularly popular. Women and children played similar ball games. All children learned to ride and horse racing was very popular. The girls also played moving camp and the boys had a type of hobby horse.

· D I D · T H E Y · L I V E · I N · H O U S E S ?

The nomadic Indian tribes, like the Blackfeet and Lakota, lived in tepees made of buffalo hide and supported by wooden poles. The tepees were put up and taken down by the women, and were easily transported by horses. Tepees could withstand the strong winds on the Plains and were warm in winter and cool in summer. Tribes who lived mostly in the same place, like the Mandan and Omaha, built earth lodges which were often much larger than the tepee. But they also used tepees for spring and summer hunting trips.

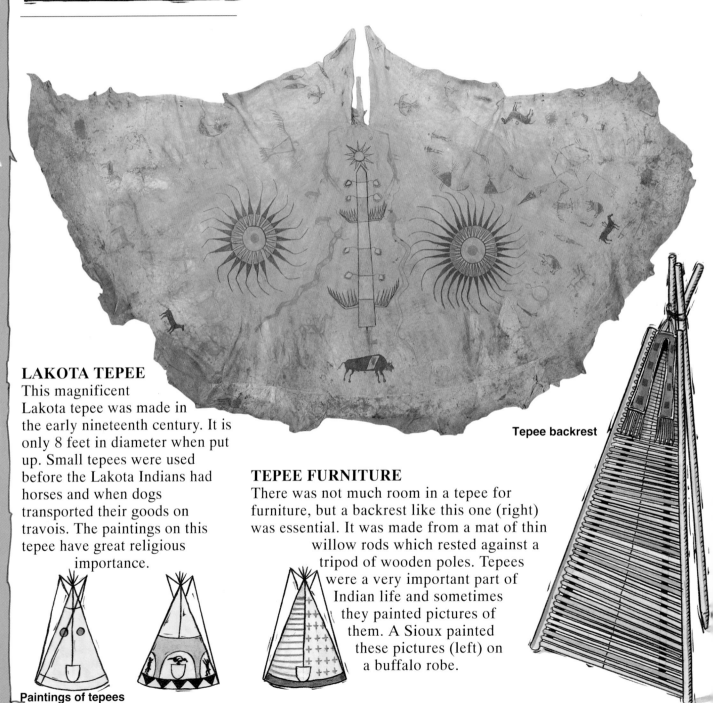

Tepee backrest

LAKOTA TEPEE
This magnificent Lakota tepee was made in the early nineteenth century. It is only 8 feet in diameter when put up. Small tepees were used before the Lakota Indians had horses and when dogs transported their goods on travois. The paintings on this tepee have great religious importance.

Paintings of tepees

TEPEE FURNITURE
There was not much room in a tepee for furniture, but a backrest like this one (right) was essential. It was made from a mat of thin willow rods which rested against a tripod of wooden poles. Tepees were a very important part of Indian life and sometimes they painted pictures of them. A Sioux painted these pictures (left) on a buffalo robe.

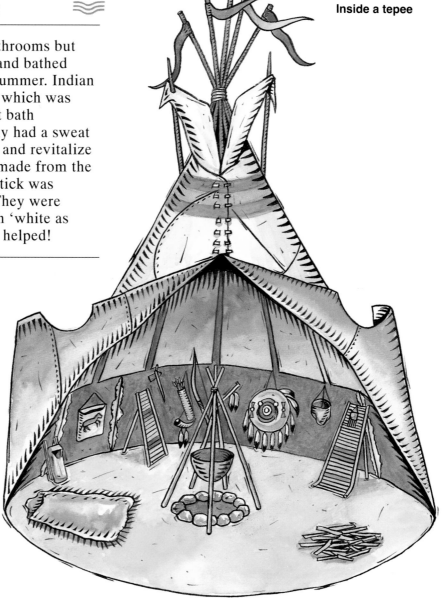

Inside a tepee

The Plains Indians did not have bathrooms but they were very fond of swimming and bathed every day in the rivers during the summer. Indian camps always had a 'sweat lodge', which was like a sauna. They believed a sweat bath 'purified' them spiritually and many had a sweat bath almost every day just to clean and revitalize themselves. They had hairbrushes made from the tails of porcupines, and a bristled stick was sometimes used as a toothbrush! They were described as having fine, even teeth 'white as ivory'. A sugar-free diet obviously helped!

INSIDE A TEPEE

The door of a tepee was a round opening which faced east towards the rising sun. In the middle of the tepee was a small fire for cooking and warmth. Indians used willow mats on supports for beds, or slept on buffalo robes on the ground. The lower part of the tepee was lined with skins to keep out drafts. The place of honor for important people or sacred objects was at the back of the tepee.

EARTH AND GRASS LODGES

Semi-settled tribes mainly lived in earth lodges (above). They were dome-shaped and covered with earth. They were 40–55 feet in diameter and for special ceremonies, 40 people or more could fit into these lodges. Grass lodges (right) were similar but only the Caddo and Wichita tribes lived in them.

· DID · BOYS · AND GIRLS · GO TO SCHOOL ?

Plains Indian children did not go to school, but they still had a lot to learn about the culture of their tribe and how to survive on the Great Plains. They learned history from story-telling and picture-writing. Ceremonies and activities, such as preparing for a hunt or war, taught them about the religion and values of the tribe, and they learned practical skills by watching and copying adults. Girls learned household tasks and needlework. Boys learned how to hunt, scout and look after horses. Both boys and girls were expert riders by the age of seven.

THE STORY-TELLER

The painting above shows a story-teller passing on the legends and folklore of the tribe to mothers and their children. Story-telling was a very important way of teaching the children about the tribe's history, religion and culture. Winters were long and cold on the Great Plains, but the tepee was made warm by extending the buffalo skin lining up the supporting poles for more insulation.

PLAINS INDIAN NAME GLYPHS

In picture-writing, Indian warriors were identified by name 'glyphs' above their heads. These men are called Whirlwind Bear and Medicine Crow. Tribes spoke different languages but most Indians understood name glyphs.

1851-52

THE WAYS OF ANIMALS

An Indian boy had to recognize and know about the animals on the Great Plains. When he grew up he would have to hunt buffalo and other animals to provide food and skins for his family. Some creatures, like the otter and black-footed ferret below, were stuffed and used to teach children about their behavior and characteristics. The Crow and Blackfeet Indians also used stuffed animals to represent their guardian spirits (see page 14) or in religious ceremonies.

SIGN LANGUAGE

Many different Indian dialects and languages were spoken on the Great Plains. In most tribes there were people who could speak more than one language, but almost all Indians learned and used sign language to communicate with members of other tribes. This was very useful for trading or making treaties. They made signs by using their fingers and hands. Look at the signs on the right and see how each one conveys the idea of what is meant rather than an individual word. It is said that you can communicate five times faster using sign language than the spoken word.

BROWN HAT'S HISTORY

Plains Indian children learned a great deal about their tribe's history from pictographs or picture-writing. The pictographs below were produced by an historian called Brown Hat. On the left, the colored patches in the circle represent blankets and other goods traded in 1851-52. In the middle, the boy with a knife above his head was killed during a raid by the Crow Indians in 1862-63. On the right, a tree has fallen and killed a woman in the winter of 1869-70.

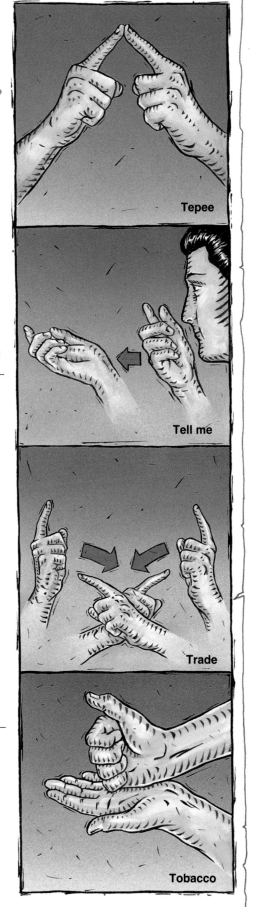

Tepee

Tell me

Trade

Tobacco

1869-70

WHAT WORK ·DID· ·PLAINS· INDIANS DO?

Plains Indian men, women and children had different work to do. A man had to provide for his family by hunting buffalo which was the main source of meat and skins and even its horns were made into cups and spoons. Good hunters were sometimes chosen by the tribal council to hunt for poor, old or sick members of the tribe as well as for their own families. After the hunt, there was lots of work for the women. They skinned and cut up the animals, because the meat had to be preserved and the hides treated. Children had work too. They looked after their younger brothers and sisters and the horses.

MAKING MOCCASINS

Women made moccasins for everyone. The tops were made of soft, tanned animal hide and the soles were made of thin rawhide which was cut to the size of the wearer's feet. The moccasins were sewn together with sinew thread and laced and tied at the front. Then the women decorated them with beads or quills in the style of the tribe. The moccasins on the right were made by the Lakota Indians.

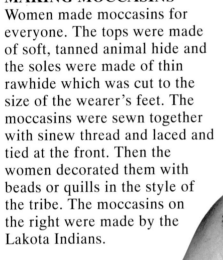

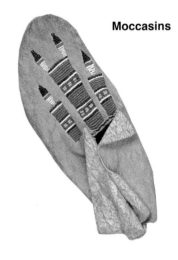

Moccasins

c

a

b

HIDE-WORKING TOOLS

These tools were used by Indian women to prepare animal skins. The skins were made into clothes, moccasins and many other items. They used the scraper (a) to remove hair from the hide. It was often made of elk (moose) horn with a flint or metal blade. The owner marked the handle to show how many hides she had tanned. The scrapers were often passed on from mother to daughter as family heirlooms. Another important tool was the flesher. It was chisel-shaped and they used it to remove the animal's flesh from its skin. Originally they were made from bone (b), but later they were made of iron (c), or with metal blades and bone handles.

MAKING PIPES

The Plains Indians made some pipes from wood, but normally they made them out of catlinite stone. Different pipes were made for different occasions, such as religious ceremonies. Women only smoked everyday pipes and young men rarely smoked because they needed to be fit. Beautiful carved pipes were made from about 1830 mainly by Sioux Indians like Running Cloud and Good Thunder, and by the Pawnee Indians. This pipe (below right) was made by a Sioux or Pawnee Indian before 1850. Today, Indian artists at the Pipestone Quarry in Minnesota still make pipes (below).

TANNING HIDES

Women tanned animal skins to make them soft and pliable. First they stretched out the hide. Then they scraped off the flesh, removed the hair and scraped the skin to an even thickness. Finally, they washed the skin, stretched it and rubbed it with a paste of animal liver and brains to make it soft.

TRAPPING EAGLES

The Plains Indians considered eagle feathers to be very valuable. They used them to decorate the head-dresses and costumes of important members of the tribe. Feathers from young golden eagles were highly prized because they were white with brown or black tips and very attractive. In the middle of the last century, just fifteen young feathers could be traded for a horse. As the eagle became an adult, its feathers changed to a mottled brown, but they were still considered valuable. Every year, families with eagle-catching skills went to places where they could trap them. They dug a pit, spread branches over it and put fresh meat on top to attract the eagles. The hunter hid in the pit and killed the bird as it came down for the meat.

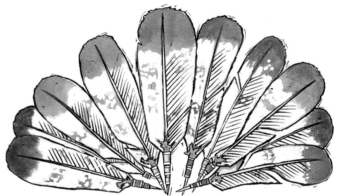

WHAT·DID THEY·DO·IN THEIR SPARE ·TIME?·

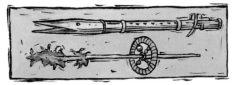

Plains Indians enjoyed many spare time activities like games, dancing, festivals and story-telling. Boys and girls learned the customs of their tribe by watching adults and making up games to copy them. Women's and men's activities were often separate. Men particularly enjoyed sports and games of chance and were members of military clubs. They dressed up and danced for different ceremonies. Many of the dances, like the Buffalo Dance, imitated animals. Women played sports too, but older women preferred to join needlework clubs.

HOOP AND POLE GAME
This painting from 1834 shows a winter earth lodge village of the Hidatsa tribe. Men of the tribe are playing the hoop and pole game which was one of the most popular Plains Indians sports. In this game of skill and chance, two men had to roll a hoop covered by a net along the ground. They threw darts at the moving hoop and scored points depending on where they hit the hoop or net. The game varied slightly from tribe to tribe. The Pawnee, for example, sometimes played the game as a magical performance for calling buffalo.

SEWING CLUBS

The women of the Cheyenne and Arapaho tribes had special sewing clubs or 'guilds'. Items like the fringed bag and vest shown below were often made in their spare time. Some kinds of quill and beadwork had religious or military importance and could only be made by certain members of the group. The quilled knife sheath made by a Cree (shown below) is probably one of these special objects. Needlework was an important pastime for Indian women and it meant they could meet socially.

FLUTES AND DICE

Flutes were popular with young Lakota men who played them to court their sweethearts. Men also played with dice which they threw into the air and caught in a dish.

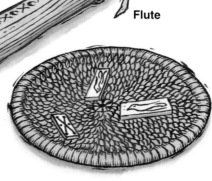

Flute

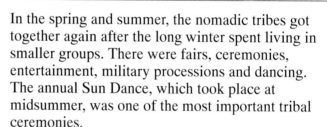

Dice

Knife sheath

FESTIVALS AND GATHERINGS

In the spring and summer, the nomadic tribes got together again after the long winter spent living in smaller groups. There were fairs, ceremonies, entertainment, military processions and dancing. The annual Sun Dance, which took place at midsummer, was one of the most important tribal ceremonies.

THE GRASS DANCE

This painting on the right from 1915 shows a Hidatsa Grass Dancer. Many Plains Indians did this dance and it had a different meaning to each tribe. For the Hidatsa it represented the life of a warrior. The name refers to the grass a warrior carried in his belt and used for lighting fires when he was on war expeditions.

W H A T · D I D · I N D I A N · · M E N · · W E A R ?

Before white traders came into contact with them, the Plains Indians made all their own clothes from soft-tanned animal skins. Antelope and deer skins were used most. Women would make and decorate clothes for everyone in the tribe. Men wore moccasins, long leggings which reached up to their hips, a loincloth and a belt. Occasionally they wore shirts, but more often they wrapped buffalo robes around their shoulders. For special occasions, everyday clothes were painted, and decorated with quillwork and hair or fur fringing. Each tribe developed its own individual style of clothes.

PEHRISKA-RUHPA

This is a picture of Pehriska-Ruhpa, an important Hidatsa Indian, from the year 1834. He is wearing a quilled shirt fringed with hair and ermine, and a buffalo robe painted with a picture of the sun. He is also holding a ceremonial pipe. His shirt was traded from the Crow Indians who were well known for making fine clothes.

EAGLE FEATHER WARBONNET

This head-dress is made of about 30 tail feathers from young golden eagles and it could only be worn by a distinguished warrior. The feathers relate to the acts of bravery by the warrior and the men he led. This style of head-dress became common around 1850 among the tribes of the central Plains, such as the Lakota and Crow.

DISTINGUISHED MEN

A grizzly bear claw necklace (right) would distinguish a very brave man in some tribes. But a man's position in his tribe was not only affected by his bravery as a warrior. His generosity, the way he treated others, or his ability to lead the tribe's elaborate ceremonies were also very important.

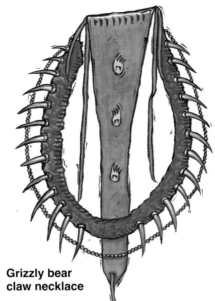

Grizzly bear claw necklace

MOCCASINS

Plains Indians wore shoes called moccasins. Each tribe had a different way of making and decorating them, but they were all made by women. The earlier moccasins were made with soft soles and decorated with quillwork. Later, the soles were made from rawhide with soft but tough buckskin tops. They were then usually decorated with beadwork. They wore out quite quickly, so when the men went on the warpath they took several pairs. The pair below are Crow moccasins and were made in the 1850s.

BUFFALO ROBES

Buffalo robes were very popular garments among the Plains Indians and to white traders too. The Crow Indians made the finest robes and traded them with other tribes. Even robes worn every day were decorated to show the courageous and generous acts of the owner, like capturing guns, taking scalps, facing the enemy and giving away horses or blankets. The robe below shows that a bow, guns, a powder horn for carrying gunpowder and a shot bag for carrying lead shot were captured by this robe's owner or his friends.

Hidatsa warrior

WHAT·DID ·PLAINS· ·INDIAN· WOMEN AND ·CHILDREN· ·WEAR?·

Before cloth was introduced in large quantities in 1870, women and girls wore dresses made from two or three deerskins. They folded the deerskin tail at the neck for decoration, or cut it off and wore a pattern made of beads to represent the tail instead. For everyday clothes, boys wore leggings, loincloths, moccasins and occasionally an undecorated shirt. They kept warm by wearing a buffalo robe over their shoulders or over their heads if it was cold. Sometimes they wore two layers of clothes in very cold weather, but the Plains Indians did not have underwear like we do. Clothes worn every day were less elaborate than the costumes made for special occasions.

Boot moccasins

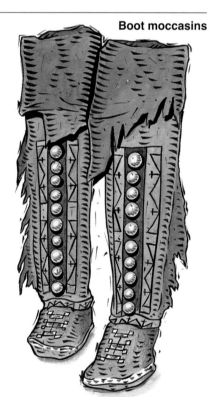

LEGGINGS AND MOCCASINS

Boot-like moccasins like those on the left were worn by women of the southern Plains tribes such as the Comanche. The buckskin tops were painted in blue and green and they were often elaborately beaded and decorated with silver buttons. On the northern and central Plains, the women wore short leggings from the ankle to the knee which were held up by garters.

Buffalo robe

CLOTH DRESSES

This Cheyenne girl is wearing a dress made of a woolen cloth traded all the way from England. The undyed edge has been used for decoration. The dress is adorned with yellow and white cowrie shells which were traded too. The shells were popular in the 1880s when dresses like this one were worn.

A WOMAN'S BUFFALO ROBE

Men's and women's robes were about the same size, but they were decorated differently. Normally men painted people, horses and other animals on them, while women's robes were decorated with geometric designs. The pattern above is called a 'box and border' design and symbolizes different parts of the buffalo.

A LAKOTA WOMAN'S DRESS

The costume on the right is called a gala dress and it would have been worn on special occasions. This one was made in about 1880 from two complete deerskins. They laced them together at the sides and sewed other seams with sinew thread. They decorated the cape with beads, colored cloth and added heavy fringes.

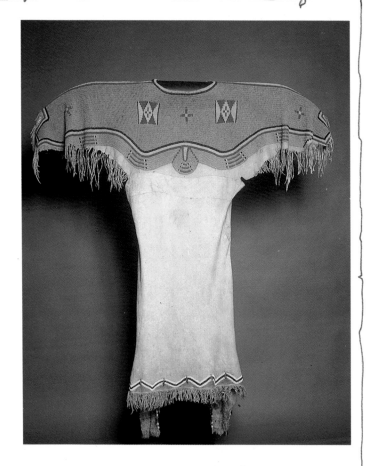

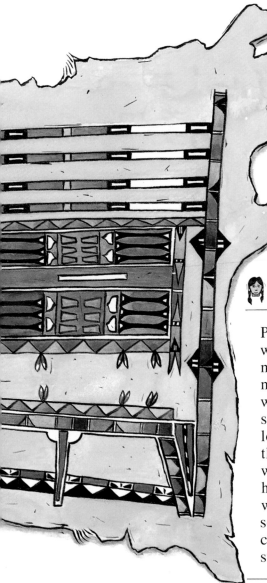

 JEWELRY AND PERFUME

Plains Indian women liked to wear earrings and bracelets made of traded sea shells or metal which were decorated with beads or quills. They sometimes wore beads in their long hair, and might also paint the parting in their hair red, which showed they could still have children. Indians did not wear perfume, but they sometimes scented clean clothes with a herb called sweetgrass.

A SIOUX WOMAN'S ROBE

The portrait on the right is of a Sioux woman called Chan-Cha-Nia-Tenin. She is wearing a summer robe which is smooth on both sides because the hair was removed from the hide when it was tanned. You can see the 'box and border' design painted in red and black with a yellow-white background.

WHAT WAS THE·PLAINS INDIANS' RELIGION?

The Plains Indians believed in many spirits. There were the underwater spirits who controlled all the animals and plants. Above the sky was the upper world which was ruled by the most powerful spirits, the Thunderbirds. When the Thunderbirds flashed their eyes and flapped their wings, they produced lightning and thunder. There was also an underworld. The Indians also believed that the spirits kept them healthy or made them ill and that they lived on after death. So the Indians honored the spirits with their medicine bundles, Medicine Pipes and religious ceremonies.

BLACKFEET MEDICINE PIPE BUNDLE

Medicine bundles, like the one on the right, contained a number of objects, such as animal and bird skins, as well as the Medicine Pipe. When someone was ill or in need, the owner, a high-ranking man, performed a ceremony to open the bundle and heal the sick person. The bundle was kept outside in the sun's rays to absorb its power.

BULL DANCE

The Plains Indians believed that buffalo had great spiritual and physical strength. The Mandan man below is performing the spectacular Bull dance as part of the O-kee-pa ceremony to make sure the buffalo hunt goes well.

THE SUN DANCE

This picture (right) taken in 1966 shows the beginning of the four-day Sun dance. The Lakota Indians were probably first to do this dance in the late eighteenth century. In part of the ceremony, the dancers tortured themselves by pushing skewers through the skin of their chest. The skewers were attached by leather thongs to a pole. The dancers asked the sun for help as the skewers tore their skin. There is evidence that the thongs were believed to transfer power to the dancers from the pole.

MEDICINE POWER

Most Plains Indian men and some women tried to contact the spirits. The most powerful was called *Wakan-tanka* by the Lakota. Less important were other powers like the buffalo, bear, the four winds and the whirlwind spirits. In times of trouble, such as war or sickness, an Indian would call on these supernatural powers to help him. This was known as medicine power. Sometimes, clothes for ceremonies and head-dresses had medicine power.

O-KEE-PA CEREMONY

The O-kee-pa was a ceremony that lasted for four days and was performed by the Mandan Indians. Men dressed up as mythical characters like the Bull Dancer shown on page 28. As with the Sun Dance, this ceremony also involved personal torture. This was meant to repay a promise made to the spirits in times of trouble, such as during a battle or when a person was ill. George Catlin, the famous explorer, was the first white man to see the O-kee-pa in 1832. When he described what he had seen, few people believed him.

MEDICINE PIPE

The Medicine Pipe below was kept in a medicine bundle. It was often called a 'thunder pipe' because, according to Blackfeet legend, the thunder gave it to the Indians as a gift. This Pipe is decorated with eagle feathers, ermine, horse-hair and an eagle head.

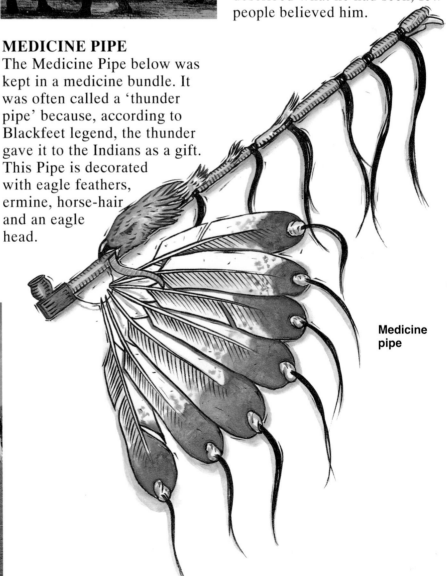

Medicine pipe

HOW DID THE ·PLAINS· ·INDIANS· ·GOVERN· THEMSELVES?

The Plains Indians did not have a government and elections like we do, but the way they governed themselves was very democratic. The important decisions were made by the 'tribal council'. Each tribe was made up of different bands and each band chose a leader to represent them at the tribal council. The men were chosen because of their bravery as warriors or for their generosity. Women did not normally sit on the council, but their wishes were very much respected and they did influence the council's opinions and decisions.

RED CLOUD'S SHIRT
This shirt, beaded and fringed with human hair, was used by the Oglala Lakota leader Red Cloud. He wore it on visits to Washington in 1872 and 1877 to represent the affairs of his tribe. The blue and yellow coloring symbolizes the sky and earth powers.

MATO-TOPÉ
Mato-topé, or Four Bears, was a famous chief of the Mandan Indians. His magnificent head-dress is made of golden eagle feathers and buffalo horns. Only very important leaders were allowed to wear head-dresses like these. The fur at the bottom of his shirt was especially left for decoration during tanning. The carved knife on his head-dress is a record of a fight with a Cheyenne chief and the feather attached to his lance relates to a successful raid against the Arikara tribe. There is also a scalp attached to the lance. This picture was painted in 1834 by the Swiss artist Carl Bodmer.

LAKOTA CHIEFS

The picture above was drawn by Amos Bad Heart Bull, an Indian historian. It shows two famous Lakota leaders – the young warrior Crazy Horse of the Oglalas who was a war leader, and Sitting Bull who was a spiritual leader. The Lakota had a council of older men called 'The Chiefs' Society' who made all the important decisions of the tribe. Other tribes organized themselves differently. The Cheyenne had four chiefs of equal rank and an elected council of 40 men to represent the other bands in the tribe.

The Sioux nation

THE SIOUX NATION

This diagram shows the structure of the Sioux Indian tribes in about 1850. One tribe is called the Teton (in the middle), which is Sioux for 'Those who dwell upon the prairies'. But the Teton called themselves Lakota. This tribe was split into seven main groups. The best known of these were the Oglala and Hunkpapa. The total population of the Sioux then was about 25,000 people.

WERE·THE ·PLAINS· ·INDIANS· ·ARTISTS?·

The Plains Indians were naturally gifted artists and their style of work was developed over hundreds of years. Almost all of their painting was done to decorate useful items like clothes, tepees or religious objects. Pipes were made of stone or wood and some of them were then carved into beautiful designs. The Indians also used their artistic skills, like rock-carving, to record historical events. Men painted, made pipes and did rock-carving, while women, who were very skilled at needlework, decorated clothes and other items with exquisite beadwork or quillwork.

SIOUX PAINTED SHIRT

This Sioux shirt was made between 1800 and 1850. The painted warfare scenes show the owner's bravery. It looks like the warriors are riding side-saddle, but they were probably painted this way to show that the horse and man are one in spirit. The man on the red horse appears to be wearing a top hat and military coat. Clothes like these were often given to important Indians at white trading posts.

PAINTING TOOLS AND PAINT

To paint an animal skin robe or shirt, the Indians first used a stick to scratch the outline of the design. Then flat sticks or a porous (absorbent) bone were used to apply the paint. These bone 'pens' worked a bit like our felt-tip pens. They made the paint from powdered earth and kept it in decorated pouches like the one below. When they finished the painting, they often covered it in a special glue to make it permanent.

Bone pens

Stick to make outline

Paint pouch

BULL BEAR'S ROBE

This robe was possibly owned by the famous Oglala Sioux Chief, Bull Bear. It is made of a very large buffalo hide measuring 6½ × 5 feet. The holes around the edge show where the hide was stretched for tanning.

Below the green horse are pictures of two warriors holding two large red disks. They are the leaders of war parties and the disks are scalps. To the right of the two warriors is a Pawnee warrior holding a red shield and on the left is a figure painted green She is probably a Pawnee woman who is being captured by the Sioux. The lively and dramatic paintings of the people are a record of some amazing acts of bravery as well as being works of art.

SCULPTURES

Skilled artists carved beautiful pipes from red catlinite stone or black stone. The traditional way to make a pipe was to drill the stone by hand using a hard stick. As the artist rotated the stick, he put sand into the hole which rubbed away the soft stone.

It took about an hour to drill a hole just 1 inch deep. The elaborate pipe below was probably made as a souvenir for military men who visited the Plains Indians.

MONTANA WARRIOR

After 1750, the Plains Indians had horses and guns and there was more warfare between tribes. The petroglyph on the right was done in Montana probably between 1740 and 1805. The warrior on horseback appears to have a broken spear. The horse was probably a war horse because it appears to have no tail. The Indians tied up their horses' tails for battle as you can see in the picture of Sitting Bull on page 31.

  ## PETROGLYPHS

Throughout the Great Plains there are many Indian pictures carved into soft sandstone rocks or on the walls of caves. The Plains Indians used flint tools to carve these pictures. They are called petroglyphs and some date back to the seventeenth century or much earlier. They tell us a great deal about the way of life of the Indians then. Before 1750, petroglyphs often showed the spiritual relationship between animals and the artist.

HOW·DID ·THEY· ·RECORD· ·THEIR· ·HISTORY?·

Most Plains Indian tribes counted the years by winters. The Sioux and Kiowa tribes in particular used a type of calendar called a Winter Count. This was made from a large piece of animal hide. Symbols of important events in the tribe's history were painted onto the skin. Some tribes may have been using this method of recording their history before they settled on the Plains. In 1879, the Oglala Chief, American Horse, said that the count he kept was started by his grandfather many years before. Other tribes did not keep counts like this, but passed on their history by word of mouth.

LONE DOG'S WINTER COUNT

The count shown below was produced by Shunka-ishnala (Dog Lone) of the Sioux. The count starts in the winter of 1800-1801. Can you see how the pictures are arranged in a spiral shape like a snail shell? At the center is the first symbol showing 30 black lines which refer to 30 Sioux who were killed by Crow Indians. Just before the last symbol is a black disk which represents an eclipse of the sun in 1869.

LITTLE BLUFF'S PAINTED TEPEE

This tepee above was given to Little Bluff, a Kiowa Chief, by the Cheyenne Chief Sleeping Bear to commemorate a peace treaty between their tribes. The black stripes on the right represent the successful war parties Little Bluff had led. Other events in Little Bluff's tribe are also recorded. Can you find the single warrior defending himself against a number of enemies? And can you see the Kiowa warrior on horseback fighting a soldier with a gun?

Some tribes used picture-writing or pictographs to record their history. Each tribe used different styles and they changed over time, especially between 1800 and 1900. The pictures on the left, probably by Blackfeet Indians, show a gun being captured (a), a warrior with a large green shield (b) and a warrior in a horned head-dress being speared (c). On the right, the Sioux pictures show a battle, a horse, and a warrior carrying a bow, arrows and a quiver. For the battle scene, the artist has painted horse hoofprints to show how the enemy in the middle was surrounded and killed.

PICTURE-WRITING WITH FRIENDS

Picture-writing was always done by men. Sometimes the man would ask friends to help him, especially if he was painting a large tepee. This way the work was done quickly and it was also a social occasion.

HISTORIANS AND TIME KEEPERS

In some tribes, like the Blackfeet and Cheyenne, historical events were handed down by word of mouth. Certain men were appointed as 'keepers' of the tribe's history. Cheyenne keepers had to promise that they would only relate tribal history with two other keepers who had to agree that it was correct.

In the Blackfeet tribe, the owner of the important ancient Beaver Bundle was also the time keeper and weather forecaster. He used sets of sticks to keep a tally of the days and months.

Picture-writing ancient symbols

DID·THE INDIANS ·TRADE?·

Trade enabled the Plains Indians to obtain goods they could not provide for themselves. The nomadic tribes who hunted the large number of wild animals in their territories did not grow many crops. So they traded their animals and skins for food like maize with the semi-settled tribes on the Missouri River. The Missouri tribes also exchanged European goods such as kettles and guns with tribes of the north-east. In this way, food, clothes, weapons and household goods changed hands all over the Plains and beyond.

THE RENDEZVOUS

At certain times of the year, the tribes would travel to great trade centers called a 'rendezvous'. A rendezvous was often named after the tribe who lived in that area. The Dakota rendezvous was on the James River in present-day South Dakota, the Shoshoni rendezvous was in south-west Wyoming, and one Crow rendezvous was on the Big Horn River in Montana. As white people made more contact with the Indians, they traded at rendezvous too. The rendezvous below took place on the Green River, Wyoming in the 1830s.

TRADE GOODS

The Hidasta shirt (right) is typical of the style made and traded in the mid-nineteenth century. The flintlock gun below was also a popular trade item. In the 1860s the Blackfeet would trade up to ten buffalo robes for a gun.

36

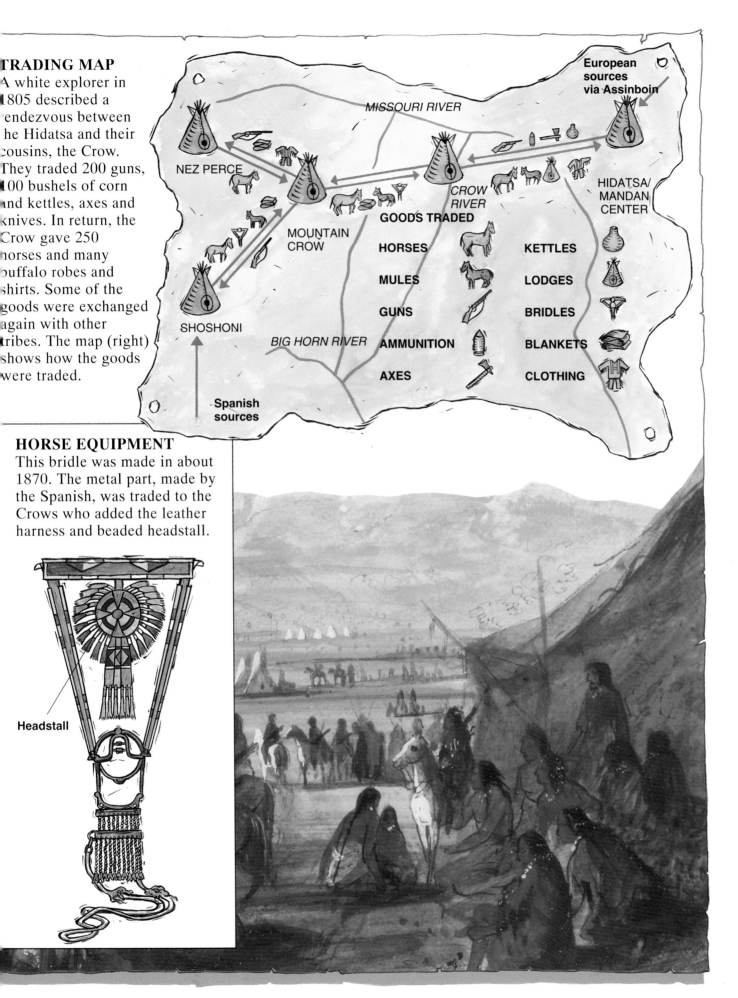

TRADING MAP

A white explorer in 1805 described a rendezvous between the Hidatsa and their cousins, the Crow. They traded 200 guns, 300 bushels of corn and kettles, axes and knives. In return, the Crow gave 250 horses and many buffalo robes and shirts. Some of the goods were exchanged again with other tribes. The map (right) shows how the goods were traded.

European sources via Assinboin

MISSOURI RIVER

NEZ PERCE

MOUNTAIN CROW

CROW RIVER

HIDATSA/ MANDAN CENTER

GOODS TRADED

HORSES   KETTLES

MULES   LODGES

GUNS   BRIDLES

AMMUNITION   BLANKETS

AXES   CLOTHING

SHOSHONI

BIG HORN RIVER

Spanish sources

HORSE EQUIPMENT

This bridle was made in about 1870. The metal part, made by the Spanish, was traded to the Crows who added the leather harness and beaded headstall.

Headstall

WHAT·WAS ·PLAINS· INDIANS' WARFARE ·LIKE?·

Before the Indians had horses and guns, there was very little warfare between tribes. In those days they used war clubs – a heavy stone attached to a long handle. After 1740, when guns were introduced, some tribes had more power and could take over new territories from other tribes. In this way, the Blackfeet and Cree forced the Shoshoni and Kutenai to move from the Plains, where they had lived for thousands of years, to the Rocky Mountains. The Pawnee also pushed the Apache west from the central and southern Plains. Even so, most warfare was for horses and few people were killed.

SHIELDS

Before the Indians had horses, they went into battle on foot carrying heavy rawhide shields (right). Shields were about 3 feet wide and had soft buckskin covers and protective amulets attached. The shield was usually painted with designs to protect the warrior. Shields were smaller when Indians rode horses in battle.

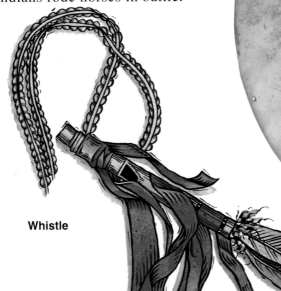

Whistle

WHISTLES

War leaders carried whistles made of eagle wingbone into battle. They were about 7 inches long and used to communicate with other warriors. Often they were engraved with lightning symbols which the Plains Indians felt would protect them.

WAR ARROWS

The picture above shows the head and shaft of a typical arrow in use about 150 years ago. The metal head was probably obtained from white traders and then bound to the shaft with sinew thread. Usually ten or twelve arrows would be carried in a quiver. The symbol on the shaft is meant to give the arrow the same deadly powers as lightning.

BOWS AND ARROWS

Wooden bows were only about 3 feet long but the arrows were 16 inches, with flint or steel heads and eagle or hawk feathers. Buckskin quivers like the one below were fringed and decorated with beads.

NO RETREAT SASH

This warrior is wearing a 'no retreat' sash. In battle, he would pin himself to the ground and refuse to move unless a fellow warrior rescued him by pulling the pin out.

 ## COUPS AND SCALPS

Most Plains Indians believed it was braver to touch an enemy in battle than shoot him with a gun or bow. So warriors might go to war with a 'coup stick', a stick used simply to strike a living or fallen enemy. The Blackfeet believed it was courageous to capture an enemy shield, weapon or head-dress. But the Lakota and Crow thought it brave to steal a horse from the enemy's camp. Scalps were symbols of conquered enemies and scalps taken in battle were always displayed for all to see. A genuine scalp included the skin and hair from the crown of the enemy's head.

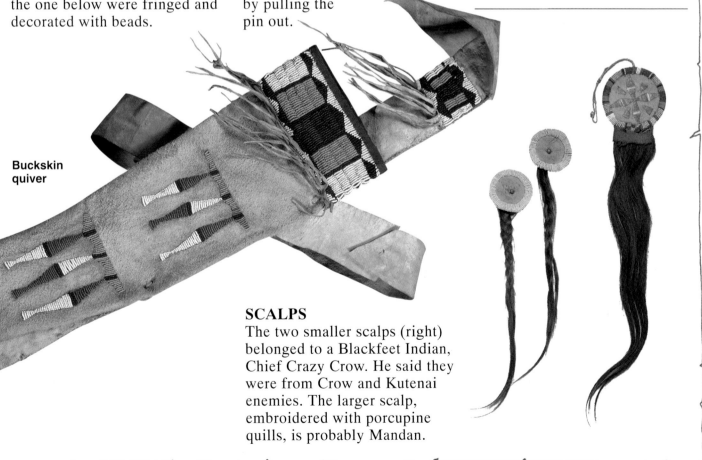

Buckskin quiver

SCALPS

The two smaller scalps (right) belonged to a Blackfeet Indian, Chief Crazy Crow. He said they were from Crow and Kutenai enemies. The larger scalp, embroidered with porcupine quills, is probably Mandan.

HOW DID THE · P L A I N S · · I N D I A N S · · C H A N G E ? ·

The Lakota called white men *wasicun* which might have meant 'one wearing bad or short clothes'! When whites first contacted the Indians they brought many useful and attractive things which improved the Indians' way of life. Blankets, knives, scissors, combs, needles and beads were all introduced, but horses and guns had the most important effect on the Indians. At first, the Indians' contact with white people was peaceful as they came to trade at fur trading posts along the Missouri River. But later the trading posts were sold to the Government and were turned into military forts.

WHITE MIGRANTS

In 1843, large numbers of white people started to migrate to the West. They traveled along the Oregon Trail every summer in covered wagons. As they crossed Indian territories, they spread diseases like cholera and smallpox to the Indians. The Indians had no resistance to these diseases and at least 30,000 had died by 1859. The settlers also killed or frightened away the wild animals. The Indians were worried that their land was being invaded, so they started to attack the wagon trains as this painting shows.

FUR TRADERS AND INDIANS

The sketch on the left was done by a Blackfeet artist in about 1840 and shows white traders and Indians. At the top, a man in a military coat and top hat and an Indian with a pipe are trading bottles, flasks, buckets and kettles. The lower sketch shows a Blackfeet wearing his traditional costume and trading for fire-water (whiskey). Can you see how his shirt fringing is shaking? This is to show the terrible effects whiskey had on Indians. They had never had alcohol until they came into contact with white people. The Indians also traded for tea, coffee and tobacco.

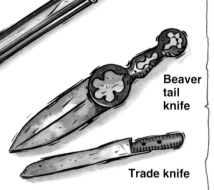

Beaver tail knife

Trade knife

GUNS

Early flintlock guns were difficult to load on horseback, so most Indians used bows and arrows until rifles were introduced in the 1870s.

Winchester rifle

Pipe tomahawk

PIPE TOMAHAWK

The pipe tomahawk (left) was very popular with the Indians, but it was invented by whites. It could be used as a pipe or weapon.

CUSTER'S LAST STAND

In 1876, the Army tried to round up the Indians who refused to live on reservations. They were known as Buffalo Indians and were led by Sitting Bull. On 25 June 1876, General Custer and the Seventh Cavalry attacked Indian villages on the Little Big Horn River. But the attack failed and Custer and his 200 men were killed. The memorial shown in the picture below is now a National Monument.

ONCE I WAS A WARRIOR

Gradually, in the last century, the Plains Indians began to lose their territory and culture as white people took over the land and killed the buffalo. The Indians were forced to live on reservations and could no longer roam the Plains freely. They tried to resist, but the massacre of 146 Indians by soldiers at Wounded Knee in 1890 symbolized their defeat. Sitting Bull's song describes how their lives had changed by 1890:

iki'cize	a warrior
waon'kon	I have been
wana	now
hena'la yelo	it is all over
iyo'tiye kiya	a hard time
waon	I have

WHAT·ARE ·THE PLAINS· ·INDIANS· ·DOING· ·TODAY?·

When the Plains Indians were massacred at Wounded Knee in 1890, they lost much of their land and their culture was suppressed for many years. It was only in 1924 that the Plains Indian people gained American citizenship and the right to vote and be elected. Now Indians are reasserting their culture and trying to regain some of their lands. In 1986, Ben Nighthorse Campbell of the Northern Cheyenne was elected to the House of Representatives and is presently the only Indian representing their interests in Congress. The Plains Indians also receive aid and money from the government's Bureau of Indian Affairs for education and to help them develop their own industries and tourism activities.

TOURIST ATTRACTIONS
Today, the Indians still produce beautiful carved ornaments and pipes which are popular with tourists and collectors.

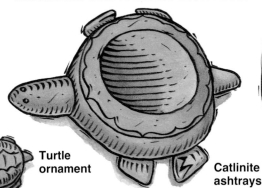

Turtle ornament

Catlinite ashtrays

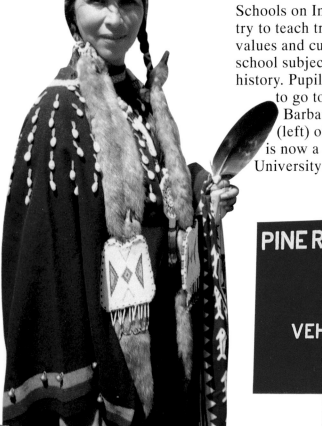

INDIAN EDUCATION
Schools on Indian reservations try to teach traditional Indian values and culture with normal school subjects like math and history. Pupils are encouraged to go to university. Barbara Feezor Stewart (left) of the Dakota tribe is now a student at the University of California.

INDIAN TRANSPORT
Plains Indians used to travel on horseback and they carried their goods on travois and later in wagons. Today, the largest reservation is about 4,500 square miles and they get around in cars or trucks. The Oglala Lakota tribe even have their own airport, shown below.

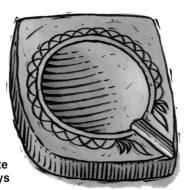

PINE RIDGE-OGLALA SIOUX AIRPORT
PINE RIDGE, SOUTH DAKOTA
DEDICATED TO THE MEMORY OF ALL VETERANS OF ALL WARS
NW—SE LANDING STRIP PAVED 60'X 5,200' LIGHTED
E — W LANDING STRIP PAVED 50'X 3,000'
PAVEMENT DESIGNED FOR 23,000—LBS. SINGLE GEAR AIRCRAFT

VEHICLES PROHIBITED ON RUNWAYS
VIOLATORS TRESPASSING BEYOND AUTO PARKING LOT FENCE
MAY BE FINED $360.00 OR 6—MONTHS IN JAIL, OR Joe E. Bluehorse Representative | G. Wayne Taplo

DO NOT DRIVE ON RUNWAYS

INDIAN POPULATIONS

Plains Indian populations often fell drastically when white people contacted them and spread diseases like smallpox and cholera. In 1837, there were 1,600 Mandan Indians, but smallpox killed so many that there were only 150 left in 1850. In 1950, the Mandan population had increased to 346. The 1990 census recorded nearly two million Indian people throughout the United States.

TRADITIONS

Plains Indians are now combining their traditional artistic skills with modern technology. Some Lakota beadwork designs have been developed using computer graphics techniques at the Little Wound High School on the Pine Ridge Reservation in South Dakota. The patterns are almost always geometrical, and these modern sneakers and the baseball cap and ball are good examples of the type of beadwork the Indians are now doing.

THE CROW FAIR

The Crow Fair is held every August in Montana on the traditional Sun-dance grounds along the Little Big Horn River. Other Indian tribes and tourists from all over America visit the fair. The Crow were famous for their white tanned buffalo hide tepees, and today they display one of the world's largest collections of canvas tepees at this fair. There are also dances and horse races for the children and a horseback parade which opens the festivities. The Crow woman above is wearing her traditional costume. Her saddle, stirrups and the horse's bridle are all typical of Crow craftsmanship.

◆ GLOSSARY ◆

AMULETS An object like a lucky charm carried by Indians after they have had a dream or vision. One amulet popular with Plains tribes was the umbilical cord, preserved after a baby was born. This was kept in a decorative pouch hung on the cradle or around the child's neck.

BUCKSKIN Softened deerskin. To make it pliable, the Plains Indians rubbed it with a mixture of softened brains and liver.

CATLINITE A soft, red stone named after the explorer and painter George Catlin. It was used to carve pipes and other objects.

COUP Touching an enemy during a battle. Generally this was considered to be braver than killing him.

COWRIE A yellow or white oval-shaped sea shell used to decorate women's clothes.

DEMOCRACY Government by the people. Popular leaders were elected by Plains Indians to represent them in council and treaty negotiations.

ERMINE White winter fur of the stoat. Plains tribes, particularly the Blackfeet and Crow, used it to decorate ceremonial clothes.

GUILD A club or society. Plains Indian women often belonged to sewing guilds.

HEADSTALL Beaded ornament for forehead of horse, attached to the bridle.

HIDE A raw, untanned animal skin.

LOIN CLOTH A strip of soft, tanned skin (or later cloth) which was worn by men between their legs; it was folded over a belt at the front and back. In battle it was considered brave to capture an enemy's loin cloth.

MEDICINE BUNDLE A collection of objects and materials which the Indians believed had spiritual power.

NOMADS People who travel from place to place, usually following animals for food.

PARFLECHE A tough bag or box made from rawhide with the hair removed. It was usually painted or decorated and the Plains Indians used it to carry food and a variety of items.

PETROGLYPH A design carved on a rock surface. Many of these are found in Plains Indian country, either on the walls of caves or exposed rock surfaces.

PICTOGRAPH Pictures painted on buffalo hides or deerskins. Some pictographs were cut on birch bark by the Plains Cree to record hunting, military or religious experiences.

PRESERVE To dry meat, fruit and vegetables. Plains Indians did this to stop the food rotting so that it could be kept for a long time.

QUILLWORK An ancient sewing technique that uses dyed porcupine quills or occasionally bird quills for decoration.

QUIVER A container for arrows. Most Plains Indians used a combined bowcase and quiver carried with a strap over the shoulder.

RAWHIDE Dehaired and cleaned hide. It is as flexible and workable as cloth when wet, but becomes hard and stiff when dry.

SINEW Thread made from buffalo muscle. The muscle was cut out in long flat strips, dried and then cleaned.

TEPEE A portable tent made of a buffalo hide cover and wooden supporting poles. From about 1870 the hide was replaced by canvas.

TRAVOIS Two long poles (sometimes the tepee poles) attached to either side of horses with a platform attached between the poles. Luggage was carried on the platform. The ends of the poles dragged along the ground.

◆ I N D E X ◆